MARGRIET RUURS *Paper Sculpture by* RON BRODA

In My Backyard

TUNDRA BOOKS

For Dick and Maeve, who host many birds and other
animals in their backyard. – M.R.

For Fred and Jean Webb, for all that they are and
for what they mean to my family. – R.B.

Text copyright © 2007 by Margriet Ruurs
Paper sculpture copyright © 2007 by Ron Broda

Published in Canada by Tundra Books,
75 Sherbourne Street, Toronto, Ontario M5A 2P9

Published in the United States by Tundra Books of Northern New York,
P.O. Box 1030, Plattsburgh, New York 12901

Library of Congress Control Number: 2006925484

Library and Archives Canada Cataloguing in Publication

Ruurs, Margriet, 1952-
In my backyard / Margriet Ruurs ; paper sculptures by Ron Broda.

ISBN 978-0-88776-775-3

1. Animals – Juvenile literature.   2. Animals – Pictorial works –
Juvenile literature.   I. Broda, Ron   II. Title.

QL49.R88 2007   j590   C2006-902091-4

ONTARIO ARTS COUNCIL
CONSEIL DES ARTS DE L'ONTARIO

We acknowledge the financial support of the Government of Canada through the
Book Publishing Industry Development Program (BPIDP) and that of the
Government of Ontario through the Ontario Media Development Corporation's
Ontario Book Initiative.

We further acknowledge the support of the Canada Council for the Arts and the
Ontario Arts Council for our publishing program.

Medium: Paper sculpture

Design: Sari Naworynski

Printed and bound in China

1 2 3 4 5 6   12 11 10 09 08 07

Welcome to my backyard!
You will see that this is a busy place – all year round.

The song of a little wren,
tail pointing up straight,
is often the first sign of spring.

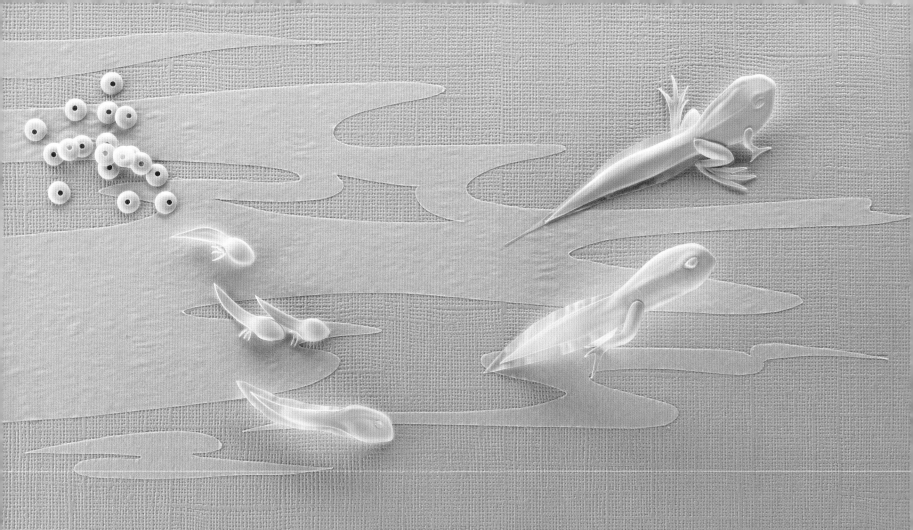

Toads find shade under shrubs by day
and call to each other by night.

6

The glistening trail of a slow-moving
snail shows me where it searched
for leaves and berries.

When spiderlings are ready to leave
home, they fly away on silvery threads.

Like a little helicopter,
the hummingbird hovers by flowers
to sip nectar.

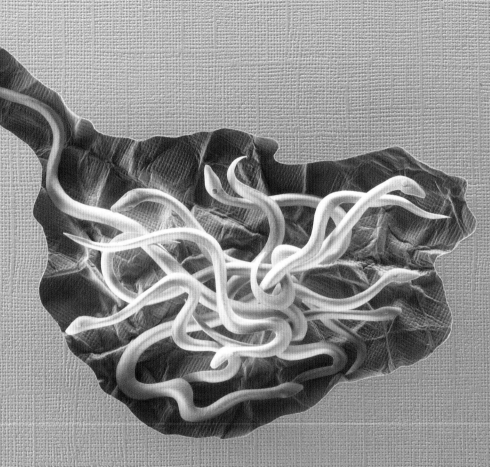

Sometimes I spot a snake slithering
through the grass, in search of
a warm place to sleep.

Like a little helicopter,
the hummingbird hovers by flowers
to sip nectar.

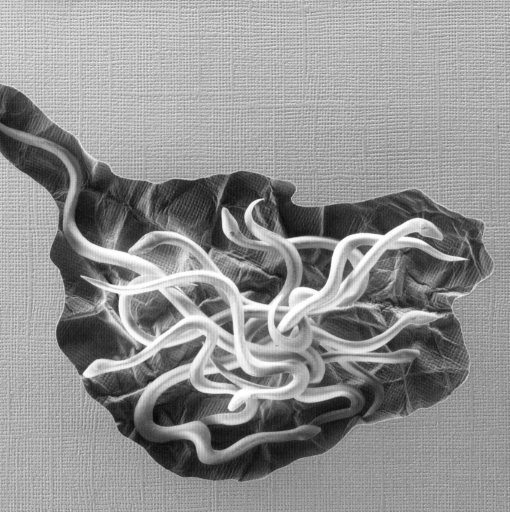

Sometimes I spot a snake slithering
through the grass, in search of
a warm place to sleep.

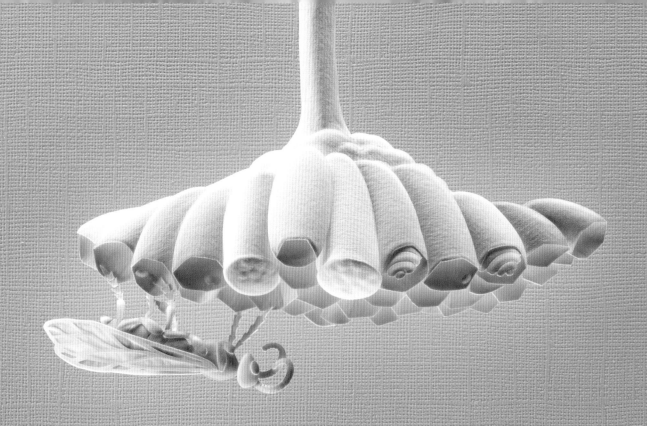

Careful not to get too close,
I watch paper wasps build a nest
for their larvae.

Five tiny swallows chatter with
excitement each time their
mama brings food.

A butterfly dances on the wind,
bringing a rainbow of colors
to my garden.

At night bats catch insects as
they soar through the sky
on silent wings.

Hungry opossums dig for peels
in our compost bin.

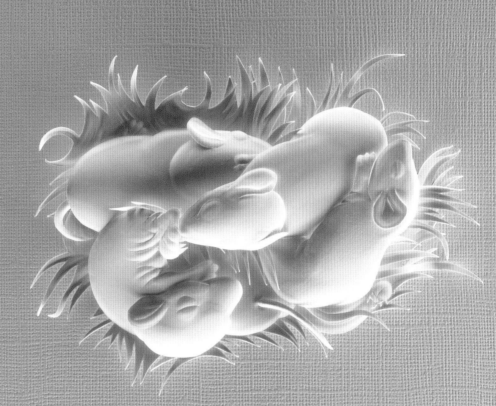

Baby mice sleep in their warm cozy
nest. When spring returns, they will
explore my backyard!

LEGEND

• *Can you find a ladybug in each double-page spread?*
• *Can you guess which animal you will meet on the next page?*
Each illustration contains a clue.

Wren (House Wren – pp. 4-5)
House wrens are small, busy birds. Despite their size, they can be aggressive. If too many other birds nest nearby, the wrens may destroy their eggs. The father wren builds a nest out of grass and twigs and lines it with feathers or fur. The mother wren lays 5 to 7 eggs and keeps them warm until they hatch. Two weeks later, the fledglings are able to fly.
Do you spot the toad on the rock?

Toad (American Toad – pp. 6-7)
Did you notice the spawn from which tadpoles are born? Tadpoles hatch from jellylike eggs laid in water. First they grow hind legs, then front legs. They start to breathe through lungs instead of gills, and finally shed their tails. The young toads leave the water, and return only to breed. Toads are mostly nocturnal, which means they are active at night.
Do you see the snail in the grass?

Snail (Garden Snail – pp. 8-9)
Garden snails evolved from sea snails. Even though they are tiny, snails are strong mollusks: they can drag ten times their own weight vertically and fifty times their own weight horizontally. The silvery trail of a snail is made of mucus, which makes the ground smoother for them to move along.
Do you notice the spider and her web?

Spider (Golden Garden Spider – pp. 10-11)
The spider spins an orb web to catch flies, bugs, and beetles. First she casts a line of strong silk, then she makes the outside frame and spins circles of silk inside it. She lays her eggs in an egg sac, often hanging it under a leaf. A young spider is called a spiderling. When it is ready to leave home, it weaves a little thread and floats away. This is called ballooning.
Do you spot the hummingbird trying to hide?

Hummingbird (Ruby-Throated Hummingbird – pp. 12-13)
A hummingbird egg is the size of a small jelly bean. Hummingbirds flap their wings at an incredible speed: 25 to 55 times per second! These tiny birds migrate to the Gulf of Mexico and as far south as Central America, where they spend the winter. They hover in front of flowers by rotating their wings in opposite directions. It is said that hummingbirds inspired the invention of the helicopter.
Do you see the snake near the fence?

Snake (Garter Snake – pp. 14-15)
Most snakes lay eggs, but the harmless garter snake gives birth to live baby snakes, as many as forty at a time. She does not stay to take care of them, so the babies look for food as soon as they are born. Snakes smell with their tongue. They have no arms or legs, yet they can move quickly and even climb trees! They have no ears or eyelids, but clear scales, called spectacles, cover their eyes. Useful in a garden, snakes eat insects that eat plants.
Do you notice the paper wasp in the distance?

Wasp (Paper Wasp – pp. 16-17)

Like an upside-down umbrella, the nest of paper wasps often hangs under the eaves. The wasps chew plant materials to make paper, then construct separate cells that each house an egg. The eggs hatch, but only the queen wasps survive the winter to start a new colony the following spring.

Do you spot the swallow in the sky?

Swallow (Barn Swallow – pp. 18-19)

Barn swallows roll and shape little mouthfuls of mud to build their nests. They lay 4 to 6 eggs, which hatch after 14 to 16 days. About three weeks later, the fledglings are ready to fly and catch their own insects. Often the parents will repair the nest and hatch a second brood. Sometimes the first brood will help to feed the new babies.

Do you see the butterfly on the morning glory?

Butterfly (Tiger Swallowtail Butterfly – pp. 20-21)

Tiger swallowtails lay eggs the size of pinheads among flowers and grasses. From these, tiny black-and-white caterpillars hatch. They eat and grow rapidly, then wrap themselves up in a chrysalis and hang from a branch. After about 10 days, the chrysalis splits and a butterfly emerges. The process is called metamorphosis.

Do you notice the bat house, where bats can safely sleep?

Bat (Big Brown Bat – pp. 22-23)

Bats are the only mammals that can fly. Bat babies, called pups, drink milk from their mother and fly in 3 to 4 weeks. A group of bats is called a colony. Bats have good hearing and reasonable eyesight. To fly at night, however, they send out high-pitched sounds, which bounce back and help them to know where objects are. This is called echolocation.

Do you spot the opossum in the shadows?

Opossum (Virginia Opossum – pp. 24-25)

The opossum (pronounced *possum*) is the only marsupial mammal in North America. A marsupial carries its young in a pouch. Baby opossums are no bigger than honeybees when they are born. They climb into their mama's pouch and stay there for 2 to 3 months. Then she carries them on her back for another 1 to 2 months, when they learn to find their own food. They use their thumbs and tails to carry things. When an opossum is frightened, it can play dead!

Do you see the little mouse in the pile of leaves?

Mouse (House Mouse – pp. 26-27)

Five or six baby mice are born in a nest, blind and hairless. After 3 to 4 weeks, they start to take care of themselves. Mice are social and curious creatures that live in close association with people. They nibble on any kind of food, including seeds, crumbs, and fruits. Mice live for 9 to 12 months.

You can invite animals to your backyard by making it an attractive place to live. Most animals need water, food, and shelter.

- Leave some grass clippings and leaves under shrubs. Animals use twigs and grasses to build their nests.
- Put out a shallow dish of clean water for toads and birds.
- Build or buy a bat house. Bats help us by eating insects that may harm plants.
- Don't use herbicides or insecticides – these will harm every animal that feeds in your garden!

Birds

- Hang nesting boxes on a fence or birdhouses in trees. Make sure cats cannot reach them.
- Build a bird feeder by setting a pie tin on a stool or flat-topped tree trunk, or hang it in a plant hanger. Fill it with birdseed.
- Make bird food by stirring 2 cups of birdseed into 1 cup of melted lard. Pour the mixture into an empty, rinsed soup can. When it has set, remove the bottom of the tin with a can opener. Insert a twig lengthwise through the lard for birds to perch on. Place a string or coat hanger in through the other end and hang it in a tree.
- Coat a pinecone with peanut butter, roll it in birdseed, and hang it from a branch.

Hummingbirds

Bright flowers attract hummingbirds to your garden. You can offer them food by filling a hummingbird feeder with a mixture of 1/4 cup sugar dissolved in 1 cup water. Do not add food coloring.

Butterflies

Butterfly bushes or shrubs with red, yellow, orange, pink, or purple blossoms attract butterflies, as do small flowers, such as zinnias, marigolds, milkweeds, and plants such as mint. Nectar-producing plants should grow in open, sunny areas. Butterflies rarely feed on plants in the shade.

Compost

No matter how small your backyard, you can always compost fruit peels, egg shells, coffee grinds, and vegetable waste. Turn your compost often. If you add dead leaves, grass clippings, and some live worms, you can make new soil for your plants!